Dr. Louise Lambert is a Canadian Registered Psychologist with almost 20 years of experience in counselling centers, mental health, non-profit organizations, higher education, and primary healthcare organizations. With a concentration in positive psychology, she has developed and delivered four evidence-based happiness intervention programs that are used still today in Canada, Kuwait, Saudi Arabia, and the UAE. With a combination of academic teaching and research, as well as consulting and private practice work with individual clients and groups, she seeks to bring positive change to individuals, organizations, and societies as a whole. Dr. Louise is the founder and Editor-in-Chief of the Middle East Journal of Positive Psychology, a journal dedicated to uncovering human excellence in the Middle East and author of two psychology textbooks, one of which explores positive psychology from a Middle East / North Africa regional perspective.

To friends and family.

Dr. Louise Lambert

HAPPINESS: GET IT, KEEP IT, OH... AND ENJOY IT!

AUSTIN MACAULEY PUBLISHERS™

LONDON • CAMBRIDGE • NEW YORK • SHARJAH

ISBN 9789948374879 (Paperback)
ISBN 9789948374886 (E-Book)

Application Number: MC-02-01-5425997
Age Classification: 17+

The age group that matches the content of the books has been classified according to the age classification system issued by the National Media Council.

First Published (2019)
AUSTIN MACAULEY PUBLISHERS FZE
Sharjah Publishing City
P.O Box [519201]
Sharjah, UAE
www.austinmacauley.ae
+971 655 95 202

Disclaimer

The information contained in this book is not intended to replace the advice, diagnosis, and treatment recommendations of qualified medical professionals. The author of this book is not liable or otherwise responsible for any reliance by you on any health information or other information found in this book – any such reliance is entirely at your own risk. Never disregard or delay seeking professional medical advice because of information contained in this book.

Miss Sunshine, You're in Good Hands...

It's official! We have a Minister of Happiness and Wellbeing in the UAE. It's a great place to live and full of human potential. We have good jobs. We have loads of holidays. We have beaches…and we have great weather (well, if you like 50+ Celsius, that is). We are a multicultural nation that is peaceful, tolerant, welcoming, and loads of fun. Yet, I bet many of you are reading this saying, yes, that's true, but why am I still not happy? What's wrong with me?

Sunshine, there's nothing wrong with you. It's that happiness is elusive, takes work, and constant vigilance, and depends upon much more than your external surroundings and personal circumstances. Sure, those play a role, but they are much smaller than you think. Happiness comes down to how we see the world, how we interpret what happens to us, how we approach problems, and on what we choose to focus. It's more complicated than just shopping (which doesn't work by the way) or spending time with friends (which does work, but you need more than that); it's a science. Really.

It's called positive psychology, the science of well-being which takes happiness as seriously as psychology has historically taken misery. The fact that we know so much about anxiety, depression, and anger shows how seriously psychology has taken its role, but the truth is, we've only just begun looking at happiness with the same vigor for the past 10 to 15 years. Being a psychologist, I'm interested in research and why things are the way they are, but I also recognize that statistics and graphs don't explain "how" someone can be happier. But, you're in luck. I was also a practicing psychologist for over 15 years and made a career out of explaining, in plain English, what those research findings mean and what you can do in turn. So, you've come to the right place if you're looking for something grounded in science. This will become increasingly important as there are "happiness specialists" popping up all over the region.

Because it is a new focus in science that seems intuitively easy compared to neuropsychology for example, everyone is trying to cash in. This book in particular relies upon empirical research (observed or experimental testing) taken from the scientific literature. Relying on the research saves you effort and avoids you wasting your money with the happiness fairy who can only seem to tell you to think positively! Duh! If that worked, we'd all be happy, wouldn't we?

I will give you practical advice from psychology and a few technical terms, but this is because I want you to know what science has to say about happiness and why certain strategies work. I don't want you to just take my word for it. I want you to learn about happiness for yourself. My commitment is to provide you with information as well as instructions to implement that information. I will also ask you questions along the way, so keep a paper and pen handy to reflect on your thoughts and feelings. I'll also give you activities to try. I am also focused on the present and future and will not be delving into your past or asking you to do so either. The past is not necessary for you to be happy today. We will also not be looking for what is wrong with you, nor will we be talking about depression. This is a book on happiness, after all!

Not Really Happy, Nor Depressed

Happiness is not a great word. For one, it has no definition in positive psychology. We prefer to break it down into positive emotions, meaning, purpose, engagement, flow, and many other states we'll see throughout this book. The word "happy" also overly simplifies the world into two camps, the cheerful unicorns (which can be so annoying), and the miserable sops who don't prance around in meadows sprinkling fairy dust on everyone. In reality, it's much more complicated. There are at least three categories of people and many degrees of intensity in between. Meet Flourishing, Languishing, and the one that needs no introduction, Depressed. As we go through each of these, decide whom you resemble most and where you spend most of your emotional time. In case you're interested, this research comes from the work of Corey Keyes.[1] I'll include all the researcher's names in case you're nerdy like me and want to read further.

Let's use a thermometer as an example. In the lower temperatures is "Depressed Mood" – the experience of negative feelings and experiences. Feeling anxious, angry, sad, depressed, or discouraged are examples. This doesn't mean that these emotions are bad, they just feel bad. Yet, feeling bad is not always bad. When you fail in a business venture, you feel like a failure and are sullen, embarrassed, or angry, but these same emotions motivate you to learn from your mistakes, try again, and succeed. The problem

---

[1] Keyes, C. L. M. (2005). Mental illness and/or mental health? Investigating axioms of the complete state model of health. *Journal of Consulting and Clinical Psychology, 73,* 539–548.

with negative emotions is when they persist beyond the duration of the actual experience or when we create them all by ourselves via our pessimistic, fearful, anxious, or self-conscious thinking. You might spend a lot of time here and it's okay if you do, this book is designed to get you out of this temperate zone and into a more positive one.

In the next section, around the zero zone, is what we call the "Languishing" zone. It's neither cold nor hot, it's room temperature. In terms of feelings, this means you're not ridiculously happy, but you're not depressed either. It's just feeling blah, sleepy, going through the motions, bored with life, or stuck in neutral. I suspect a lot of us are here, in fact, it's where the majority of people find themselves. They just "are".

Finally, up in the positives are "Flourishing" people who experience positive emotions and experiences. They are not only happier, they function better too. The flourishing have good close relationships (real ones, not 872 Facebook friends they've never met!) and are satisfied with work. They have a sense of purpose in life and feel that it's worthwhile. They tend to be in better health and use fewer prescription medications. They even think more effectively than those in the less positive zones of the thermometer (more about this later). We call them flourishing because they are actually growing.

Imagine our thermometer goes from − 10 (depressed) up to zero for languishing and proceeds to the +10 for flourishing. Think about where you spend most of your time and perhaps not where you are at this minute which might be really low if you're going through a bad moment or really high because you're extra happy today. Write down your number here.

Most of the time, I am at: ________________________

This number will be your benchmark for growth, so don't worry if it's lower than you'd like. It'll increase.

What Now?

Happiness takes work. Some strategies I'll offer you, you will like more than others. All rely on your efforts, but doing these activities once and then forgetting about them is no more helpful than going to the gym once. You have to keep it up until it becomes part of your lifestyle. On the other hand, obsessively focusing on happiness and forcing yourself to be happy will be about as effective as only eating carrots, making you tired, resentful, and greatly annoying to those around you! A better way is to try each strategy twice to see how it feels and if it's not your thing, then it's not. There's many, you'll find one that fits. You should look at doing these whenever the mood strikes or about once or twice a week, otherwise it becomes a job and a punishment and I can think of nothing worse than to be punished with happiness! Blech!

But first, let's see where you are at.

Why do you want more happiness?

Why do you want it now? Has anything happened to make you focus on happiness at this point in life?

How do you want to be different? Be specific.

Is Your Software Working?

Think about when you are happier. This may be a challenge as it may have been a while ago or just today. It doesn't matter. Your answers will provide clues as to what you need to adjust to make happiness more likely.

When am I happier?

What creates that happiness?

What specific role do you play in that? How do your actions and thoughts make that happiness more likely?

What exactly makes you happier: is it the event or how you are at that moment?

If you came up with even one example, it means your "happiness generator" works. Phew! But, did you notice that you had a role to play in your happiness? Happiness doesn't *happen* to you, we create it by being open and interacting with people, situations, activities, and our own thoughts to create it. You could win loads of money and a trip around the world but if you're closed, they won't matter. You make situations come alive with happiness by what you do, how you respond, think, and how you interpret situations. You might be good at doing that in some places and less in others. That's okay. Happiness takes practice.

Rate your ability to make happiness happen for yourself (that's called your self-efficacy). Don't worry if it's not as high as you want, I'll ask again at the end of the program, it'll be higher for sure.

1	5	10
I'm awful at making happiness happen.	I can do it sometimes, I just don't know how I do it!	I'm awesome and know how to keep it there.

If you have 4 or less, I'm glad you're here and you'll change your mind soon enough, but why do you think you're bad at this? What evidence do you have for this belief? Is it easier to believe you can't, so if it fails you won't be disappointed? Share.

If you have 5–7, think about the times where you have made happiness happen, how did you do that? What helped create those moments? How were you different?

If you're in the 8 and above zone, well done! Share how you make happiness happen and keep it.

Involve Others...!

Now is the time to introduce happiness to your social circle by asking people when they are happier. You can do it over coffee, dinner, while driving, at work, or with your kids or parents. Be prepared for laughter, strange looks, and blank answers! Ask 10 people. Go do it now; write it down and see what patterns you find.

Did you notice that happier times usually do not involve a new car, television, or shoes (although people might say that to be funny or because they feel these things should make them happy)? Usually, answers involve time spent with others, using one's skills, learning, travelling, or engaging in activity. Other moments might be smaller, like sitting on the beach, exercising, or coloring with kids. Happiness is not usually found in objects, even though as a society, we continue to value material things as though they were a measure of our worth. Where we focus has consequences for happiness; more on this later.

Why Is Happiness the Better Choice?

In these next sections, I'll give you the reasons why more happiness is better, but it's likely you don't need much convincing. Researchers[2] reviewed hundreds of studies and showed that better health, relationships, and money lead to greater happiness, but they found more evidence showing that happiness acted as a magnet pulling success toward individuals. People who were happier first were more successful in their jobs, likely to secure interviews, get good performance reviews, and show higher performance and productivity. They even earned more money and were better liked by others. They were more involved in their communities and had better relationships. Happier people had better health behaviors and stronger immunities, and experienced greater physical health. They solved problems with more creativity and flexibility too. It turns out that as happier people experienced and expressed more positive emotions, they were more likely to be successful.

You might think happier people are more successful because they have more resources in the first place. It's possible. But the research suggests not; happiness comes before successful outcomes and causes success.[3] In sum,

---

[2] Lyubomirsky, S., King, L.A., & Diener, E. (2005). The benefits of frequent positive affect. *Psychological Bulletin, 131*(6), 803–855.

[3] Seligman, M.E.P., Steen, T.A., Park, N., & Peterson, C. (2005). Positive psychology progress: Empirical validation of interventions. *American Psychologist, 60*(5), 410–421.

happy people are more successful in health, income, employment, and relationships because of what they do, how they think, and because of the people and situations they attract. They also benefit in terms of the freebies they get because of how others perceive and respond to them.

Bigger Smiles, Longer Lives

When we experience negative emotions, changes occur in the body that in the short-term are not harmful, but in the long-term can be. Under the influence of negative emotions, our bodies become flooded with stress hormones like adrenaline and cortisol (among others). For instance, if you meet a snake, the boost of adrenaline is very welcome and gives you a shot of energy, raises your heart rate, narrows your pupils, interrupts your digestion, and limits your thinking so that survival is the only thing on your mind. Yet, when faced with long-term stressors like fighting with our spouse, lacking in life purpose, or worrying about bills, these same effects are not conducive to health and a constant state of emergency interrupts daily functioning, overworking the immune, cardiovascular, and lymphatic systems, as well as sleep patterns.

Happier people bounce back quicker from stressful events and generate lower amounts of stress hormones; in fact, positive moods decreased cortisol by 32%![4] Positive emotions and states like optimism are associated with better immunity (higher natural killer cell activity and more helper

---

[4] Pressman, S.D., & Cohen, S. (2005). Does positive affect influence health? *Psychological Bulletin, 131*, 925–971; Steptoe, A., Wardle, J., & Marmot, M. (2005). Positive affect and health related neuroendocrine, cardiovascular, and inflammatory processes. *Proceedings of the National Academy of Sciences, 102,* 6508–6512.

T cells)[5] and play a role in reducing stress and wear on the body.

Positive emotions also contribute to people enjoying better health and living for longer. In the famous "Nun Study", researchers[6] read a large number of autobiographies nuns had written 60 years prior to joining the convent and looked for positive emotions and indicators of a positive approach to life, as well as negative emotions. They found a strong association between the positive emotional content of the autobiographies and health and longevity sixty years later.

Positive moods also increase social support, physical activity, and self-care, while decreasing stress. People who experience more positive emotions are more likely to engage in things like basketball, walking, or cycling, and more likely to get their cholesterol and blood pressure checked, as well as their prostate exams and mammograms done.[7] Happier people are more physically active and smoke less;[8] they also sleep better.[9]

*Before you blame unhappy people for their illnesses, remember that medical conditions are affected by what you do (i.e., obesity, smoking, and lack of exercise), but are also affected by environmental or genetic causes. Being happier stacks the deck in your favor, but chance, environment and genetics do the rest.

---

[5] Salovey, P., Rothman, A.J., Detweiler, J.B., & Steward, W.T. (2000). Emotional states and physical health. *American Psychologist, 55*(1), 110–121; Segerstrom, S.C., Taylor, S.E., Kemeny, M.E., & Fahey, J.L. (1998). Optimism is associated with mood, coping, and immune change in response to stress. *Journal of Personality and Social Psychology, 74*(6), 1646–1655.

[6] Danner, D.D., Snowdon, D.A., & Friesen, W.V. (2001). Positive emotions in early life and longevity: Findings from the Nun Study. *Journal of Personality and Social Psychology, 80*(5), 804–813.

[7] Ibid 2.

[8] Martin, M. W. (2008) Paradoxes of happiness. *Journal of Happiness Studies, 9*(2), 171–184.

[9] Pressman, S.D., & Cohen, S. (2005). Does positive affect influence health? *Psychological Bulletin, 131*, 925–971.

Altered Thinking

Positive emotions create broad[10] or more open thinking and allow us to take in more of the environment. When we tune in to the present, we focus and pay attention, but when preoccupied with negative thoughts or focus on the future or past, we filter out and miss positive opportunities.[11] What you focus on becomes your experience. Many studies[12] have shown that positive emotions help improve attention, boost creativity, and increase flexibility in the face of problems; they make us more concerned about others too. They increase our ability to think in more abstract ways and help

---

[10] Fredrickson, B.L., & Branigan, C. (2005). Positive emotions broaden the scope of attention and thought-action repertoires. *Cognition and Emotion, 19,* 313–332.

[11] Rowe, G., Hirsch, J., & Anderson, A. (2007). Positive affect increases the breadth of attentional selection. *Proceedings of the National Academy of Sciences, 104*(1), 383–388.

[12] Kok, B., Catalino, L., & Fredrickson, B. L. (2008). The broadening, building, buffering effects of positive emotions. In S. J. Lopez (Ed.), *Positive psychology: Exploring the best of people* (Vol. 3, pp.1–19). Westport, CT: Greenwood; Fishbach, A., & Labroo, A. (2007). Be better or be merry? How mood influences self-control. *Journal of Personality and Social Psychology, 93*(2), 158–173; Isen, A.M. (2003) Positive affect as a source of human strength. In L.G. Aspinwall & U.M. Staudinger (Eds.), *A psychology of human strengths: Fundamental questions and future directions for a positive psychology* (pp. 179–195). Washington, DC: American Psychological Association; Labroo, A. & Patrick, V. (2009). Providing a moment of respite: Why a positive mood helps seeing the big picture. *Journal of Consumer Research, 35*(5), 800–809.

us persevere at tasks and take on goals with increasing difficulty and complexity. Under the influence of positive emotions, we even have better memory. This is why depressed people complain of not being able to remember things; their brains are flooded with adrenaline and cortisol, which narrow their focus, but also during overthinking, it's hard to remember or focus on what you were doing in reality.

The Cash Is Better!

Like you needed another reason! In a meta-analysis[13] of 286 studies, income was strongly associated with happiness. Those who experience greater positivity were more likely to increase their income and chances of promotion, as well as report fewer periods of unemployment.

Why? Let's say you had to hire someone and had two candidates. Both were equally educated and with the same level of skill and experience. One shakes your hand, makes eye contacts, smiles, and says, "I am so pleased to meet you and I'm really looking forward to this interview." The other simply says, "Hello," and avoids eye contact and smiles little. Now, I know you will say, maybe they are both equally happy and you might be correct, but outwardly, which person is showing it?

Demonstrations of happiness do not guarantee a better hire, but they can be good clues because we know that happier people are more sociable, think better, have better memories, are in better health, are more creative, productive, and so on. This would suggest that the happier person would be more efficient, profitable, use less sick time, be a better team player, add to office morale and thus, be more appealing to employers. So, keep that in mind the next time you go for a job interview, but remember to keep it real and appropriate. Fake or over the top happiness doesn't fool anyone.

---

[13] Pinquart, M., & Sörensen, S. (2000). Influences of socioeconomic status, social network, and competence on subjective well-being in later life: A meta-analysis. *Psychology and Aging, 15,* 187–224.

Librarians Will Like You!

Happier people tend to have more social connections[14] with all types of people like the librarian, neighbor, their kid's teacher, or grocery cashier. All of those relationships count and add richness to life. If you don't believe me, say hello, ask how someone's day is going and wish them a better one, and notice how you feel afterwards. You might not feel amazing, but your mood probably improved if only because you've escaped your internal mental whirlwind for a moment. Happier people are more likely to know and be known by others, form groups, and even volunteer, socialize, or be otherwise engaged in social groups like monthly Art Movies, photography clubs, and badminton. They have meaningful interactions with others, big or small, and feel that they belong. These connections bring important benefits.

Happier individuals have stronger interpersonal trust[15] and use relationships to share life's difficulties and joys. By trusting others, they expect positive responses and

---

[14] Fredrickson, B.L. (2002). Positive emotions. In C.R. Snyder & S.J. Lopez (Eds.), *Handbook of positive psychology* (pp. 120–134). New York, NY: Oxford University Press; Fredrickson, B. L. (2004). Gratitude, like other positive emotions, broadens and builds. In R. A. Emmons & M. E. McCullogh (Eds.), *The Psychology of gratitude* (pp. 145–166). New York: Oxford University Press.

[15] Burns, A.B., Brown, J.S., Sachs-Ericsson, N., Plant, E., Curtis, J., Fredrickson, B.L., & Joiner, T.E. (2008). Upward spirals of positive emotion and coping: Replication, extension, and initial exploration of neuralchemical substrates. *Personality and Individual Differences, 44,* 360–370.

consequently, get it. Happy people take social risks by introducing themselves first, making eye contact, and initiating conversation. They have faith that if they receive a negative response they'll survive. Less happy people tend to be less trusting, take fewer risks, and are often preoccupied with themselves and their thoughts to the point of not noticing others. They may expect things to turn out poorly and do not bother trying. As a result, others do not invest the effort either.

Happier people are also more knowledgeable as a result of their social connections[16] and benefit from vast stores of information the less connected have no access to. They know where the job openings are and who is selling a dining room table for cheap. They even gain favors, something that is always useful.

Finally, the freebies which happier people obtain as a result of who they are, how they think and act, and who they draw into their lives is another benefit. We just like happy people and act differently towards them. We judge them as more physically attractive, appealing, intelligent, and competent, as well as warm, friendly, and assertive. Whether true or not is beside the point; it's that we assume it is and act accordingly. Thus, happier people cash in on the stereotypes that people have about them. Being happy is important for its own sake, but it is also important at a social level as there are distinct benefits to people knowing you are happy.

In the end, it is not fair, but people are more likely to want to be friends with and give support and assistance to people with a positive outlook.[17] It's true, the depressed person needs the support the most, but this is the way it works. The next time you are out in any group, notice who gets the support or attention. It might be the loud guy in the room, but look more closely. Are people attracted to him because he is happy?

---

[16] Ibid 13 (Fredrickson, 2002).
[17] Ibid 5 (Salovey *et al.*, 2000).

What will change for you when you become happier? Think about work, relationships, social life, activities, health, etc.	What are the negative consequences to being happier? How might your family, friends, children, or partner respond?

What might other people notice about you when you are happier?

Don't Kill It!

You don't do it on purpose; it sneaks up on you. At first, you innocently review situations, conversations, other's actions. Then, you ruminate on your feelings, repeat the same phrases, and mentally watch the same scenes like a movie. Next thing you know, your good mood is gone. Too much thinking kills happiness![18]

The brain automatically processes events and situations. This is good in that you don't need to concern yourself much with finding solutions as it'll happen by itself while you're busy with other things. But, other times, we try to force-feed the solution mechanism by overstuffing it with problems. It's like pressing the "Help" button on your computer over and over; do it enough and your computer will freeze or crash. Of course, not all thinking is bad. Considering a problem is how we deal with emotions, find solutions, and make sense of life. It helps us move forward. But, too much thinking becomes overthinking and it's not useful.

What does your overthinking sound like?

---

[18] Lyubomirsky, S., & Tkach, C. (2003). The consequences of dysphoric rumination. In C. Papageorgiou & A. Wells (Eds.), *Rumination: Nature, theory, and treatment of negative thinking in depression* (pp. 21–41). Chichester, England: John Wiley & Sons.

When does it become useless; how do you know it's gone too far?

Like Brushing Your Teeth

Overthinking encourages the very feelings you're trying to get rid of; like a headache, the more you focus on it, the more intense it becomes. Plus, maybe you've heard of "paralysis by analysis"? Overthinking leads to confusion about which direction we should take and moves us further away from solutions because we can't think straight. The more we do it, like brushing our teeth, the more it becomes a habit. Overthinking also stops us from being in the moment, such that something good might be occurring, but we are deep in thought and miss it.

How do you minimize or stop your overthinking? Think of times you've overcome it, even for a few minutes, what did you do? Remember, I'm not asking about when you should have faced a problem but didn't want to, but about overthinking that has negative consequences for your thoughts, actions, and emotions.

Overthinking is a problem for positive situations too. When we over-analyze and try to determine why good things happen, they lose their mystery and delight. If someone did a good deed for me, I can appreciate it instead of thinking about what they might want from me. I can just be thankful and move on.

Do you overthink positive events? How does that work out for you? What happens to your joy?

Here are some ideas for reducing overthinking. After each, comment on how they might work for you and find ideas of your own. Ask others how they deal with overthinking. This is critical; once you reduce your overthinking, there will be more space for the introduction of positive emotions and experiences.

Idea 1: Do something physical: walk, run, play squash, do some stairs, row, stretch. Physical efforts force you to breathe, interrupt your thinking, and clear your mind by reducing stress hormones. How would this work for me?

Idea 2: Write it out. But use order. What is the exact problem? What is my role in it? What can I do to solve it (even if I don't want to)? When, how will I do it? How can I prevent it from happening again? Be strategic; don't just review emotions. How would this work for me?

Idea 3: Get busy, but play music or television in the background to prevent you from fully thinking. It might be dishes, folding clothes, organizing a bookcase. Put time between the event and your thoughts so your feelings can settle down. How would this work for me?

Idea 4: Respond to your overthinking like an external audience would. I say – "Stop it, you're doing it again" and do ideas 1, 2, or 3 until the time is right to think calmly. Don't overthink your overthinking though. Just notice, stop it, and move on. How would this work for me?

Idea 5: Be purposeful and plan the day. This won't stop immediate overthinking, but it'll put order to what you do and prevent some issues from occurring. Plan your stress responses ahead of time to remove the need to overthink. How would this work for me?

Other ideas:

Other ideas:

Other ideas:

Mindfulness; Attach Your Head to Your Feet!

You may have heard about mindfulness;[19] it's all the rage. There's many ways to understand it, here's my favorite: Keep your head attached to your feet! Let me explain…

You're sitting here reading this book. Yet, your thoughts might be elsewhere. Your head has disconnected and it's travelling to the past thinking of events from 2009. The more you think of them, the worse you feel and other bad memories pop up too. You've read the last four sentences several times, but didn't register any of them. At times, your head goes the other way, it worries about things it thinks are coming but haven't happened and you're in 2021 and feeling anxious. You've lost connection to today. Your feet are here but, by themselves, they're useless because your head is not.

How often and how much time do you spend in a day being disconnected from your immediate reality?

---

[19] Brown, K.W., Ryan, R.M., & Creswell, J.D. (2007). Addressing fundamental questions about mindfulness. *Psychological Inquiry, 18*(4), 272–281.

Does it help?

When we disconnect, we are mindless. The brain does not focus on the immediate present, but focuses inwards and creates an internal story that is neither real, nor reflective of the actual chronological time. We create a lot of our own stress by mentally replaying negative events that are long gone. It's tough to stay in the present where most often not much is happening, but we need to train our minds to do that more often.

I have been through some terrible things in my life, some of which actually happened.
Mark Twain (1835–1910)

Can You Drive a Car?

Think of mindfulness as the ability to keep a car on the road instead of losing control and driving over curbs and through stop signs. So, if you can keep a car on the road, you can think of the future (a little worry is okay as it helps us plan and set goals) and the past, but only if you can focus on the positive or perhaps the negatives if there is a purpose and in small doses. If you can't, sorry, hand over the keys and practice some more; you'll get in an accident otherwise. Here's how to do it.

Notice the external

Sitting here today, at this time, notice what's happening around you. What do you hear? A car driving by, neighbors, a bird, the hum of lights, air conditioner, silence? What do you smell? Dust, fragrance, laundry soap? What do you see? A door, chair, blanket, desk, the street? What do you feel against you? A pillow, couch, a bench, or sandy beach? While focused on these things, here and now – are you okay?

Maybe you've got a toothache that made you say no, but generally people say yes when they reflect on the immediate moment. We need to be in the present to not get stuck in the past or future and create turmoil for nothing. There are enough road hazards in life; you don't need to create more on your own.

When you notice that you've travelled to the past for no reason or are imagining future events that might happen but probably won't, come back to the present by asking these questions. Try it!

What can I see?
What can I smell?
What can I touch?
What can I physically feel against/on me?
What can I hear?
What can I taste?

Fatima uses mindfulness at breakfast because by 8am, she is usually stressing over her daily 3pm staff meeting even though she knows it achieves nothing and makes the day longer and more miserable. Now, she preserves her morning sanity by focusing on her breakfast (taste, smell) and book (tactile, thought), and worries about the meeting an hour before. If your day is going to be bad, why make it worse and for longer?

Will mindfulness make you happy? No. But, we need to clear some mental space to give happiness a chance. You can't feel happy if you're busy worrying or being sad at the same time. Use mindfulness as needed, it takes a few seconds and no one will notice what you're doing.

Practice your mindfulness this week and write about it in the next section. Don't move ahead until you do, otherwise you'll just be reading about happiness and not actually living it. See you in a few days.

Driving School Practice!

This week, try mindfulness three tries and write about it. Remember not to get frustrated; you'll only cause overthinking! And by the way, it likely won't work the first time, the second time you'll forget, the third will happen for 10 seconds. Be patient, happiness involves retraining the brain, just like learning a new language.

Attempt 1: Date, time, and what happened:

Attempt 2: Date, time, and what happened:

Attempt 3: Date, time, and what happened:

If you were successful, what was the result of using mindfulness?

You've had three tries, what seems to work well and what makes mindfulness more difficult?

You've been reading this book for a while now: how have your thoughts and actions changed so far?

Matchmakers Agree; Fewer Is Better!

Maitha wants to get married, so her friends, aunts, mother, and cousins start interviewing potential mates. Tall, short, muscled, rich, intelligent, well-traveled, and interesting men, how to choose? Each is as good as the next, only different! But, every choice made means one is also rejected. Maitha finally chooses Omar. He's great, but knowing there were other good options makes her feel as though she might have made a mistake even though nothing says that she did.

This is the Baskin Robbins effect (like the ice cream), where too many options make us unhappy because we have knowledge of what we could have had, but didn't choose. Further, the other options end up creeping into mind when things go bad. The first moment Omar and Maitha have troubles, she'll think I should have picked Suleiman! Yet, if she hadn't known about Suleiman or the others, she'd be happier with Omar.

When it comes to making decisions, people either satisfice or maximize.[20] When *satisficing,* they set minimum standards for what they need to be happy, i.e., tall, funny, and once they reach that, they make a decision and stop there. They limit their options once they reach "good enough" and make it work after that.

In contrast, less happy people *maximize* and consider all the options and try to make a perfect decision creating an impossible scenario as their options are endless, tiring to

---

[20] Schwartz, B. (2000). Self-determination: The tyranny of freedom. *American Psychologist, 55*(1), 79–88.

organize, remember, and rank, as well as take too long. It also makes comparisons more likely, guaranteeing that we find something better and become unhappy as a result.

Are you a satisficer or maximizer?

How well do these work for you?

Think of a decision you are facing now or in the near future and consider your minimum standards so that you know when to stop looking. This might be for a new job, buying a house, or even choosing your next holiday. Apply satisficing more often and see what happens. List your standards here.

I need_________________________________ to be happy in this
area of my life:

42

*You might have more than three standards, but you'll
only spend longer without the situation you want and be in a
state of wanting. You'll also have to decide whether some
things really matter (if you want a partner for example), like
height. Wouldn't kindness be better? Finally, it's one thing
to demand things, but remember that others will demand
things from you too.*

Happier People Don't Care as Much

Miriam got a work promotion! Hana is pleased for Miriam and thinks of how she can celebrate, maybe take her to lunch. In contrast, Saeed congratulates Miriam, but wonders why he didn't get a promotion? He is just as good and considers this unfair. He was having a good day, but ruined it by comparing himself to Miriam.

Measuring our success against that of others is a recipe for feeling bad because there is always someone doing better, moving along faster, or with a very different situation. Maybe she got lucky in a family business, or married well. Maybe she worked hard, maybe not. Feeling bitter about other's success stops you from moving ahead and keeps you stuck in the negative. Happy people know this and care little about the success of others in the sense that they do not use the good news of others to decide whether they are successful themselves.[21] They use their own standard for that.

Do you compare yourself to others?

---

[21] Abbe, A., Tkach, C., & Lyubomirsky, S. (2003). The art of living by dispositionally happy people. *Journal of Happiness Studies, 4,* 385–404.

How does it make you feel?

What are the consequences of self-comparison?

Might you need to change these mental comparisons? What can you do, think of, or tell yourself instead?

Happier People Force Themselves

Hamdan and Hameed got in a car accident. They suffered broken bones and had to take time off work. But, how each responded was interesting. Hameed got depressed and thought about how much worse it could have been. He was upset at having to go for physiotherapy and become angry with people who tried to help. Hamdan was also shaken by the event, but vowed to become physically stronger and looked forward to going to physiotherapy as until then, he hadn't been taking care of himself. And even though he was off work, he arranged to do some work from home, only 2 hours a day, but enough to keep himself busy. He invited a friend every day to keep him company too. Instead of being defeated, he decided to improve his life.

Happier people look for the good in the bad and do it on purpose[22] because it's neither easy, nor obvious to find good in a car accident. In case you're wondering, happy people are sad when bad things happen and respond like everyone else, but they force themselves to look for positives as a way to move forward.

---

[22] Lyubomirsky, S., & Tucker, K. L. (1998). Implications of individual differences in subjective happiness for perceiving, interpreting, and thinking about life events. *Motivation and Emotion, 22,* 155–186; Abbe, A., Tkach, C., & Lyubomirsky, S. (2003). The art of living by dispositionally happy people. *Journal of Happiness Studies, 4,* 385–404.

How about you? Are you easily defeated or do you give yourself permission to feel bad for a time and then purposefully focus on the positives to move ahead?

If you're more like Hameed, how could you refocus on the positives? In fact, try it now, is there something you could think about differently to help you move forward?

Is there a situation from the past that still bothers you? Could you re-evaluate it by focusing on what good came from it? There is always something good that comes from the negative, even if it is only more life appreciation and a renewed sense of purpose. Rewrite the situation here, but from the positive this time.

Don't Blame Me!

Years ago, a study[23] was conducted with people who'd won a lot of money and another group who'd become recent paraplegics. At first, the winners were happy spending money, but by three months, their happiness levels returned to normal and they were no happier than non-winners. In fact, the money made it harder for them to like the things they used to. They assumed that with money life is full of excitement, but you still have to discipline your kids, exercise, talk with your spouse, and fill the day with something productive.

On the other hand, the paraplegics were miserable at having lost physical functioning and had to make tough adjustments. They worried about things like relationships, adapted transportation, work prospects, and daily living. At three months, their happiness levels were still low, but by six months, they were almost back to normal. It took them longer to adapt, but the fact that they did says we adapt to negative life events too.

What can we take away from this? One, circumstances don't matter much over time because we get used to them.[24] This means that circumstances, the things that happen or don't happen (like not getting the job you want), are not a good place to look if you want something to blame or

---

[23] Brickman, P., Coates, D., & Janoff-Bulman, R. (1978). Lottery winners and accident victims: Is happiness relative? *Journal of Personality and Social Psychology, 36,* 917–927.
[24] Lyubomirsky, S., Sheldon, K.M., & Schkade, D. (2005). Pursuing happiness: The architecture of sustainable change. *Review of General Psychology, 9*(2), 111–131.

equally, if you want to change your life because we *adapt;*[25] we get used to things, both good and bad.

The fact that we adapt, habituate or get used to things, is both good news, as well as bad news. Bad news as it means you'll get used to positive changes quickly and even faster when the changes are superficial, and you'll have to keep adding challenge and opportunities as a result so that the emotional impact of good things does not fade with time. On the other hand, adaptation is really good for bad events and means that if you just wait, the emotional sting of bad events will eventually not be felt as strongly.

Do you tend to blame your circumstances for your unhappiness? How does it work for you?

On the other hand, do you look to external events to make you happy? How does this work for you?

How long does it take you to adapt to the good? What can you do to increase this time so that the effect of good things can last longer?

---

[25] Lyubomirsky, S. (2011). Hedonic adaptation to positive and negative experiences (pp. 200–224). In S. Folkman (Ed.), *Oxford handbook of stress, health, and coping* (pp. 200–224). New York, NY: Oxford University Press.

You're Not Spending It Right!

You're still not convinced about the money issue? Okay, it is more complex than that. If you can't meet basic needs like food, clothing, and housing, money will make you happier, but beyond that, it doesn't add much to happiness because we adapt to money too and in the face of more only find other ways to spend it.[26] Yet, if you can meet your needs, how you spend money becomes important.

Investing in experience, such as going on a holiday, as opposed to objects like shoes is more effective in generating happiness.[27] Not convinced? We both go to Vienna and my trip is done cheaply, but I have loads of fun and talk to all sorts of random people and have crazy experiences! Yours may be highly luxurious but lonely and really boring. Money doesn't guarantee anything. Further, investing in material goods is the weaker option as goods can be lost, broken, or surpassed by newer models. If you link happiness to things, you might even begin to think objects define you. Having money isn't bad; it's what you do with it that counts.

---

[26] Diener, E., & Biswas-Diener, R. (2002). Will money increase subjective well-being? A literature review and guide to needed research. *Social Indicators Research, 57,* 119–169.

[27] Van Boven, L. (2005). Experientialism, materialism, and the pursuit of happiness. *Review of General Psychology, 9,* 132–142; Van Boven, L., & Gilovich, T. (2003). To do or to have? That is the question. *Journal of Personality and Social Psychology, 85*(6), 1193–1202.

Whether you have a lot or a little doesn't matter, are you more focused on experiences or objects?

Which has been more meaningful for you in the past? Which has led to greater growth and positive experiences?

We've had a lot to think about; how about we move into something fun? After all, isn't that happiness?

Take a Break and Take Some Pictures!

We have much good in our lives but due to adaptation, the fact that we get used to good (and bad) things, we fail to see it. This activity[28] will help you look at your life with new eyes. Here's how.

Taking photos, whether we go back and look at them or not, forces us to stop and notice details that we take for granted, and consider the significance of what we see. Photos also help us imprint scenes to memory. Yet, we only do this on holiday; why not every day?

Pick a morning, afternoon, or evening and experience your usual surroundings like a tourist. Notice plant growth, interesting architectural angles, scenery, meals, movement, birds, or your regular morning walk. Force yourself to find and appreciate something new. Collect your photos and save them in a folder. You can even make a video. Every month, pick a slice of time and document it. You'll enjoy the present more and build memories for later. You can even have your kids join you in this activity and make a folder for themselves or as a family.

---

[28] Kurtz, J. L., & Lyubomirsky, S. (2013). Using mindful photography to increase positive emotion and appreciation. In J. F. Froh & A. C. Parks (Eds.), *Activities for teaching positive psychology: A guide for instructors* (pp. 133–136). Washington, DC: APA.

Report on how it went, but, for now, decide on which day you will do this. ______________________

Where will you go?

With whom?

How did this activity work for you?

It's Better Than You Think!
(Really)

Naming three good things is a way to find and focus on the positives. Studies[29] show that if you take time to find three good things out of your day every day, it can keep depression away as you are always looking for positives. You can write about it each day in a happiness journal too; it just can't be the same three things each day. You can even use this as a subject of dinner conversation with your partner, children, or friends.

Sometimes people can't find good things. In that case, focus on the bad events that could have happened but didn't. For instance, I did not experience a hurricane, drought, or civil war today. People experience these things all the time. Today, you did not. Sometimes, the absence of a negative is all you'll get. It counts too.

Note your three good things for today and then continue finding three good things for the next few days.

Today: three good things…

---

[29] Ibid 3.

Day 2:

Day 3:

Day 4:

Day 5:

Day 6:

Boring Bit Alert!

It wouldn't be a psychology book without theory, would it? But, you've understood it all so far, this will be no different. In the PERMA[30] model, there are five routes you can pursue to achieve happiness. You don't need to pick just one, you're probably already using many, but they help to understand why and how certain actions and thoughts lead to happiness. I've noted the pathways below. Read and see which you use most by scoring yourself from 1 (never) to 10 (always). Then, in the right column, describe how you use this pathway and rewrite the description for yourself. All pathways are good and relying on one doesn't mean you don't do or care about the others; it's a preference. All of the strategies we use from now on will fit with these pathways.

---

[30] Seligman, M. E. P. (2011). *Flourish: A visionary new understanding of happiness and well-being.* New York, NY: Free Press.

PEMRA Pathways		Rate 1–10. 10 is high	If I were to rewrite this pathway for myself, how would it sound for me?
Positive Emotions and Pleasures	I love enjoying myself and delighting in pleasures on a daily basis whether it's laughing, enjoying a good meal, savoring my kid's laughter, buying myself shoes, or listening to music, watching the sunset.		
Engagement and Flow	I often and easily lost myself in difficult activities like scrap booking, playing tennis, doing research, solving crosswords, collecting stamps, or in activities that others think I spend too much time doing.		
Relationships	I care deeply about my family and friends. I call them often and spend as much time with them as I can. If they are sad or need help. I try to help or just sit with them. My social circle means		

	everything to me; I would choose them every day over activities. I find my happiness in others.		
Meaning	My values, beliefs, or religion matters. When I decide to spend time doing something, I consider how it fits my purpose. I do the right thing. Morals are vital. I think about how I live my life; what it means. I know what I am here to do.		
Achievement	I always set goals and see how much I can achieve and what I can make happen for myself. I like to see how far I can push myself and what I am made of. I love the feeling of succeeding, meeting my goals and immediately setting new targets!		

Pathway of Positive Emotion

The Cadbury's secret unveiled!

In positive psychology, a formal definition of happiness does not yet exist in the same way it does for depression. Nonetheless, one theory states that happiness is the experience of positive emotions gained from gratifications, things that give instant positivity, like receiving a hug from a child, or smelling freshly baked Uum Ali. The broaden and build model[31] is included in the pathway of positive emotion as it explains what positive emotions do and why they are useful. But first, list as many positive emotions as you can:

That's tough to do because we pay so little attention to positive emotions and much more to negative ones. But, whatever you wrote in your list is an example of a moment of happiness. According to the broaden and build model, you get an injection of happiness any time you experience a positive emotion. With happiness defined as the occurrence

---

[31] Fredrickson, B.L. (2006). The broaden and build theory of positive emotions. In M. Csikszentmihalyi & I.S. Csikszentmihalyi (Eds.), *A life worth living: Contributions to positive psychology* (pp. 85–103). New York: Oxford University Press; Fredrickson, B.L., & Joiner, T. (2002). Positive emotions trigger upward spirals toward emotional well-being. *Psychological Science, 13,* 172–175.

of any positive emotion, happiness is far easier to identify and create.

Let's put it otherwise. Say we have a scale of 1 to 10 and happiness is a 10. This sets the bar very high to start and means that we only accept happiness as the times when there are disco balls, confetti falling from the sky, kittens, and rainbows. I don't know about you, but if this is happiness, I'm miserable!

It does not mean that 10s don't occur, they do and might be the day you get married (or divorced!), have a baby, or graduate from university. Most people will have less than a handful of 10s – that's why they are so special, they are rare, and if we had many, we wouldn't appreciate them as much.

What about the moments below 10? We often overlook them, but happiness is also the 1, 3, and 5's of life. When we change the definition of happiness from a 10 to the smaller positive emotions (the numbers below it), the frequency with which we experience happiness increases. In other words, you're likely much happier than you realized. We've had the wrong definition all along!

Yes, positive emotions are short-lived, but they build long lasting resources by affecting our thoughts and actions. They broaden thoughts and change how we see the world; we are more creative, flexible, and better problem solvers. Broadening in turn, builds four categories of resources that are useful now and later. They are:

Cognitive: we gain knowledge, information, and skills useful for problem-solving in school and work, and are more likely to see opportunities for ourselves.

Psychological: we gain self-esteem, self-efficacy, and confidence from our activities and interactions.

Physical: we engage in health-related behaviors (i.e., sleep, exercise, healthy eating) and our stronger immune systems help us live longer.

Social: we make more connections and friends that provide trust, support, fun, mutual cooperation, knowledge, and help with coping.

New definitions, new emotions

We all want happiness to be the 10 and dream about it happening to us all the time like a shawarma delivery. But isn't it also freeing that you can make moments below 10 happen every day? Share your thoughts.

How do you feel about the new definition of happiness? Is it disappointing? Is it a relief?

So, what are the positive emotions anyway? Inspiration, love, gratitude, curiosity, interest, vitality, joy, hope, pride, amusement, serenity, and awe are just a few. Here's a description of many of the positive emotions which will be helpful.

Pleasure tells us that an activity, situation, or engagement is rewarding; yet, not all pleasures are good for us, like smoking. Pleasures are nonetheless important and when not harmful, reduce stress, increase our coping capacity, encourage sociability, and impact our health positively[32]. For instance, physical pleasures like stretching, holding a child's hand, hugging your partner, or running provide instant pleasure. *Contentment* helps us to savor life and offers insight about the world and our role in it.[33] Pleasure is more immediate and stems from a situation, while contentment comes from contemplating life and is more deeply felt.

Vitality is the experience of feeling alive and happens when you are physically fit and psychologically well and includes a sense of purpose and meaning.[34] It's related to physical health and a sense of agency (feeling like you can act on your life and make things happen) and self-actualization (reaching goals and becoming our best selves). I experienced vitality when I trained for marathons. I had

---

[32] Veenhoven, R. (2003). Hedonism and happiness. *Journal of Happiness Studies, 4,* 437–457.

[33] Ibid 13, Fredrickson, 2004

[34] Ryan, R. M., & Bernstein, J. H. (2004). Vitality: Zest, enthusiasm, vigor, energy. In C. Peterson & M.E.P. Seligman (Eds.), *Character strengths and virtues: A handbook and classification* (pp. 273–289). Oxford: Oxford University Press.

energy, felt strong, happy, focused, determined, and knew exactly what my purpose was. Vitality is the overlap of mental and physical health; thus, exercise and physical activity play an important role here.

Curiosity is the feeling we get when we recognize something of interest and pursue it.[35] We generate new behavior, focus our attention, explore new things, and change our view of the world as a result. We grow from the experience of curiosity. *Inspiration* consists of three parts, transcendence, meaning that we attend to something bigger than our usual life concerns; evocation, meaning inspiration happens and cannot be planned; and motivation, a desire to do something.[36]

Awe[37] also involves anything experienced as larger than one's self, as well as the mental changes that occur in response to what was unknown until then. In the face of awe, we respond with passive submission, attention, and imitation resulting in it being transformative. Closely related is *elevation,*[38] an emotion we experience as a result of witnessing kind and selfless acts. It is moving, uplifting, and triggers us to be more pro-social as we feel a desire to help, love, and be closer to others.

Gratitude is the awareness of others goodness that is directed at us.[39] By recognizing that positive events are due

---

[35] Kashdan, T. B. (2004). Curiosity. In C. Peterson and M.E.P. Seligman (Eds.), *Character strengths and virtues: A handbook and classification* (pp.125–141). New York: Oxford University Press/Washington, DC, American Psychological Association.

[36] Thrash, T. M., & Elliot, A. J. (2004). Inspiration: Core characteristics, component processes, antecedents, and function. *Journal of Personality and Social Psychology, 87*(6), 957–973.

[37] Haidt, J., & Seder, P. (2009) Admiration and Awe. Entry for the *Oxford Companion to Affective Science* (pp. 4–5). New York: Oxford University Press.

[38] Algoe, S., & Haidt, J., (2009). Witnessing excellence in action: The other-praising emotions of elevation, admiration, and gratitude. *Journal of Positive Psychology, 4,* 105–127.

[39] Emmons, R. A., & Mishra, A. (2012). Why gratitude enhances well-being: What we know, what we need to know. In Sheldon,

to the kindness of others, we see ourselves as receivers of generosity and feel more positive emotion. Gratitude is recognizing that somebody went over and above the call of duty for no other reason than because they wanted to do something for us. Through this, we recognize that we are important.

Optimism involves thoughts, feelings, and motivation that helps people move ahead with challenges.[40] It can involve an outlook on life (i.e., human nature is good), or challenge (i.e., how long will I wait at the bank?). It is indeed a form of self-deception that motivates us to close the gap between reality and an outcome, but also reflects a sense that life will bring good things in the future. *Hope* concerns the images of the actions required to achieve goals.[41] High-hope people think of many goal pathways and believe in their ability to reach them.

Finally, *pride* is experienced when we consider success the result of our efforts.[42] Pride can extend to others too. We can feel pride watching athletes at the Olympics, your child's poetry competition, or friend's graduation. Pride leads us to persevere on tasks especially when others can recognize our efforts[43] and encourages us to reach more achievements. Some people think pride is bad; if it's used to make others feel negatively, then yes, but, pride can signal

---

K., Kashdan, T., & Steger, M.F. (Eds.) *Designing the future of positive psychology: Taking stock and moving forward* (pp. 248–262). New York: Oxford University Press.

[40] Peterson, C. (2000). The future of optimism. *American Psychologist, 55*(1), 44–55.

[41] Snyder, C. R. (2002). Hope theory: Rainbows of the mind. *Psychological Inquiry, 13*, 249–275.

[42] Tracy, J. L., Weidman, A. C., Cheng, J. T., & Martens, J. P. (2014). Pride: The fundamental emotion of success, power, and status. In Tugade, Shiota, & Kirby (Eds.), *Handbook of positive emotion* (pp. 294–310). New York: Guildford Press.

[43] Williams, L.A., & DeSteno, D. (2008). Pride and perseverance: The motivational role of pride. *Journal of Personality and Social Psychology, 94*(6), 1007–1017.

that you've done something good and is a result of positive living.

It's good to recognize positive emotions so that you can acknowledge them when they occur. Be mindful though as positive emotions are weightless and short-lived. Catch them when they arise and see if you can't savor and stretch time to make them appear more intense.

How do positive emotions affect you?

How would others say you are different under the influence of positive emotions? What do they notice?

Let the Count Begin! The Positivity Ratio

While pleasures are easy to get, they are not enough to assure happiness over time. This is due to the fact that positive emotions weigh little and as a result, disappear quickly. In fact, compared to negative emotions, we need three of them to offset one negative emotion.[44] Thus, we should be on the lookout for positive emotions and savor them to get the benefits of broadening and building noted above. Notice that there is room for negative emotion (it's three to one, not three to none), so you don't need to remove them; instead, simply increase the positive ones to increase the gap between them. Track your positivity ratio: think of today and recall how many positive emotions you've experienced compared to negative ones. Write it here.

_______________ : _______________

positive emotions   negative emotions

Tracking your ratio many times a day can help you notice how much time you spend in the negative. The aim is to increase the number on the left, so don't worry about the number on the right. Do this a few days in a row to see if you are in the languishing or no growth zone, or the flourishing zone, and see what you can do about it.

---

[44] Fredrickson, B. L., & Losada, M. (2005). Positive affect and the complex dynamics of human flourishing. *American Psychologist, 60*(7), 678–686.

Gorillas or Macchiato?

I'd been wanting to go to Rwanda for years to see the mountain gorillas. There are only 800 of these gorillas left in the wild in the whole world. It's a famous area, think Dian Fossey, Gorillas in the Mist. That's the spot. I finally did it after years of anticipation. We had two weeks for a break and living in Dubai, I was able to take one week for Rwanda, the next for Vienna. I hadn't really planned much for Vienna, it was just someplace to go. But, everyone I spoke to about Rwanda responded the same way, oh, lucky you, it'll be amazing, I'm so jealous! I was so excited to go I could barely sleep the night before!

When I got there, it was pretty cool. Kigali is amazing, clean, and orderly; people are kind, everything is so green and lush, and did I say, clean? By far, the cleanest country I've ever been to and that's a lot.

But, it was also exhausting, maybe I was tired. We hiked, hiked, and hiked. Beautiful scenery, gorgeous and I felt privileged to see the landscape. On the day we went to see the Visoke crater, it was insanely muddy, it rains a lot, and the mountain is steep. We had climbing poles, but they were useless as we had to grab on to vines and roots to pull ourselves up. Doing this for a few hours got me major blisters on both hands. People fell repeatedly, myself included, caked in mud, luckily, it was thick and gooey, we fell slowly, but still. One woman sprained her elbow and had to come down. The mood was low. I've trekked before and run marathons, but this really tested my patience. It went on all day. Then, the altitude hit. I got nauseous, dizzy, and got lost on the mountain. Yep. I started to cry, I was so disoriented and our guide was already at the top sunbathing!

I was talking to myself, had to stop several times to catch my breath and I just couldn't. If you've ever had altitude sickness, you'll know the only remedy is to come down in altitude, but I didn't want to be separated from the group, so I kept climbing. Oh. I was panicking.

I go to the top and lay there being very unhappy and hoping to puke thinking it would make me feel better. The volcano was beautiful but I couldn't enjoy it. When I look at photos of it now, I don't remember being there. The experience was overshadowed by the mud and altitude sickness and the return trip down.

We saw the gorillas the next day, more trekking, and that was truly was amazing. It was a highlight for sure that stands out in my memory, small babies, mammas playing, the large silverback farting and scratching himself. I felt like I was in their living room watching them chill for the evening. The trekking resumed until the moment I got back on the plane.

In contrast, Vienna was easy. I had many a macchiato people watching. I went to museums, concerts that moved me and brought tears to my eyes, I love the cello and violin. I sat in beautifully manicured gardens and took so many photos I used up all of my camera's memory! It was sunny; I read a book on the grass. As far as experiences go, Vienna was filled with many positive ones. Yet, when you ask me about both, I *evaluate* Rwanda as amazing (which it was), but also because I feel I should. It was far away, expensive to get there, a lot of hard work, and yet, very meaningful and moving, especially on the day we visited the Genocide Museum. I would recommend it to anyone. But, in terms of *experience*, actual moments of positive emotion, there were many more in Vienna.

There is a difference between how we evaluate what we do, in other words, how we feel about something, and how we actually experience it.[45] My experiencing self in Rwanda

---

[45] Dolan, P. (2014). *Happiness by design: Change what you do, not how you think.* New York, NY: Plume. Kahneman D., & Riis J. (2005). Living, and thinking about it: Two perspectives on life.

was suffering, but I evaluate it exceptionally high. My experiencing self in Vienna was positive, light, and optimistic, but my evaluation was a bit lower, after all, everyone goes to Europe. We do things that are pleasurable but perhaps not very meaningful (a macchiato is pleasant but not a soulful experience), and we also do things that are intensely meaningful, even transformative, and that have many negative emotions attached at the same time. Which is best? We need both types of experiences.

See how much time you spend in positive emotion by filling in this chart. Be honest and consider whether the activity brings *you* positive emotion, because sometimes an activity brings others positive emotion and we think we should feel the same way. How many times have you been pulled to an expensive, "to die for, must go to be seen" restaurant that is overpriced, average, and uninteresting, but that everyone is pretending to love? You might say it was great to fit in, but your experiencing self knows better. Ten dollar water, really?

The chart will help you consider what is pleasurable for you and what you might do more often. And if you're like me, it might just be reading a book. Don't be ashamed of what you like. Do it for a few days to get an idea.

In F.A. Huppert, N. Baylis & B. Keverne (Eds.), *The science of well-being* (pp. 285–304). Oxford: Oxford University Press.

My Positive Emotion Generators

Day	Before work	Morning until noon	Afternoon until dinner	Evening

Activities that consistently bring in positive emotions:

Are there things that you experience positively but evaluate negatively? For example, I get pleasure from doing housework, but I'm not "supposed to", so I don't tell anyone.

Are there activities in which you spend time that you evaluate positively (i.e., fancy restaurant), but don't in fact experience positively?

Thinking of the last question, why do you suppose you engage in activities that bring you no joy?

What might you do differently as a result of this activity?

Remember When...?

This activity is useful when you have nothing good to focus on or anything to feel good about. After all, not every day is great; some days are bad and others neutral. Either way, there is room to increase the ratio.

Mark had a revelation when he did this exercise. He chose to recollect his wedding day which took place in the 1970s. It was in the church and he was at the altar waiting for his bride. He was wearing white pleather shoes, the kind that make your feet sweat. His suit was white polyester and he had a blue blouse underneath it with a frilly opening. He even described his perm! After a few moments, his bride began to come down the aisle and he thought he was going to faint because he was so nervous. He remembered her huge dress, curly tendrils by each side of her head, and blue eye-shadow...he recalled at that moment thinking, "Martha is the love of my life! I can't think of anywhere else I would rather be than right here." He got tearful and broken voiced as he told us and we did too. But, what came next was profound. "We divorced about two years later, but it doesn't take away from the fact that I was happy that day. Since then, I hadn't felt that sort of happiness ever. I'm thankful to know what that felt like, because some people have never felt love like that..."

How something ends does not take away from the fact that it was.

This week, get in the habit of thinking and writing about your positive experiences.[46] Describe the scene and the feelings; what came before or after is not relevant. Just focus on the moment. Positive moments do not last long. You'll only have a few lines, but you will re-experience and reap the benefits of that positive emotion once more. Make sure to only write about the time itself, not what came later or how it disappeared or ended badly. Take your time. When done, consider how you feel thinking of that moment? Did your ratio increase? Share your memory with someone or write about all of the positive emotions over several days or weeks. The more activities you do, the more positivity becomes a habit.

---

[46] Bryant, F. B., Smart, C. M., & King, S. P. (2005). Using the past to enhance the present: Boosting happiness through positive reminiscence. *Journal of Happiness Studies, 6,* 227–260.

Savor Your Latte!

I can drown my latte in a matter of minutes while scrolling on my iPhone, or I can focus on its taste, texture, and smell and actually enjoy it. While I love lattes, sometimes I multitask and ignore its experience as a result. What I should be doing is savoring, noticing the steam rise up from the cup, imbibe the caramel and strong smell of coffee, and letting the creaminess of the non-fat version melt in my mouth! I'm doing it anyways, why not enjoy it?

Savoring[47] is another way to generate positive emotions and involves appreciating and extending positive experiences. By taking in the details of what we see, hear, smell, taste, and feel, we can build memories to recollect later. We can savor a walk in the park, food, classical music, or crossing things off a to-do list. It takes no extra time or effort; savoring only requires you to notice what is already there to a greater extent.

Savor at least three moments this week by attending to pleasure and be present in your experiences instead of focusing outside watching traffic or ruminating on negative thoughts. Be where you are. We are surrounded by moments of pleasure and goodness all day long, but need to attend to them in order to benefit.

What do you currently savor?

---

[47] Bryant, F.B., & Veroff, J. (2006). *Savoring: A new model of positive experience.* Mahwah, NJ: Erlbaum.

What can you savor today more closely? Think of three more things from your usual routine that you can begin to savor more. What are those three things?

Expect the Best!

People think optimism is being silly, naïve, and blind to the realities of life, but so is being cautious, skeptical, and mistrusting! Optimism is not about pretending reality doesn't exist; it is choosing a mindset for success.

Imagine you're going for an interview. You doubt it will work out. This low mood saps your energy, makes you seem glum, and promotes overthinking and self-doubt to the point where you respond to questions poorly. You give the impression that you couldn't be bothered. Surprise, you don't get it! Not because you couldn't have, but because your pessimism caused you to act and think in a way that brought out the worst in you. Try again. You're hopeful, smiling, and funny; you expect this to work out. You're open to conversation, paying attention, and conscious of putting your strengths forward. Whether the job works out or not isn't the point, it's that optimism promotes success by changing your behavior and thoughts and increases the likelihood of success.

Think about a situation you are (or will be) facing and develop three optimistic beliefs and/or actions like in the situation above. You may have a quote or saying to remind you that the future will be brighter, or a song you play to put you in a good mood. If there is no current negative situation, do not create one! One will come along soon enough, so don't go to the future and get it. Instead, note how you use optimism now and see if you could improve it for the purpose of getting the best from yourself.

Pathway of Engagement

Are you a spectator or a player?

Engagement is about participating in life and not only watching it. It involves our interest and attachment to the activities in which we spend a lot of time and feel are important. If they were taken away, we'd feel lost. These activities can be the violin, football, writing a novel, or painting a work of art that relies on our character strengths (like perseverance, organization, initiative, love of beauty, etc.), physical, and mental efforts, as well as zest, the energy and excitement we bring. When we commit to activities and become good at them, we are rewarded with a state of flow, a feeling of absorption I'll describe later, as well as greater meaning in life. We also reinforce our character strengths by exercising them repeatedly. The key to engagement though, is time. These activities aren't done once, but repeatedly over months and years. As Aristotle said, excellence is found in the habits we do.

List the activities in which you spend a lot of time outside of work and family life that use your talents, strengths, effort, and energy, and that you've been doing for some time.

If that was tough, don't be discouraged! Engagement is the most difficult pathway and one that people avoid because it involves effort and a risk of failure. Yet, it is the most powerful pathway for growth and hits back against depression more than the others. So, if you're feeling like you don't want challenge, keep reading anyways! You'll learn why these activities are good for you and how not to give up when they become hard.

Why hard is better.

We have an aversion to hard work these days, one our grandparents wouldn't recognize. We have lives of convenience, maids, nannies, drive-through banks, McDonald's and dry cleaning! We barely move anymore and that's a tragedy as we lose opportunities to develop our character strengths and build excellence. Doing easy stuff doesn't exercise the body, mind, or character strengths, but hard stuff does.

We also have the idea that anything unrelated to work, family, or friends is immature. Many of my students report being told by their parents that sports is for kids, art is for primary school, music is for bohemians! Wrong. These activities are where we learn to be great. Take sports, it's where we use our character strengths to cooperate, accept losses, discipline ourselves, learn about, and control our bodies through good nutrition and sleep, surpass our mental limits, and strive with opponents towards excellence. Where else do we get opportunities to learn these things?

Think about the times you did something difficult. How did it help you grow? What skills did you use? What did you learn and how did you feel about yourself after you did it? Do easy things teach you this much?

I know you've dreamed of doing something amazing and tough. Maybe you've never shared it with others because it seemed too hard. Go on, write it here. If your effort, talents, zest, and time were guaranteed, what's something difficult you'd like to do? Maybe climb Mount Everest, play the saxophone, speak Mandarin?

What's your plan? Optimism isn't enough!

Haitham wants to improve his fitness, but has done nothing for nine years. He got on a treadmill and tried to run. He took off really fast and lasted 27 seconds! He was embarrassed and went home. Sound familiar? It's not enough for Haitham to believe he can do something; he needs a plan to get there. How?

First, he needs to change his expectations. He has been sitting for years. It's not going to happen in 27 seconds! All good things take time; yet, he can realize small gains quickly if he plans it right.

Second, starting fast won't work. He might do a slow jog or a fast walk for 30 seconds and see how he feels. If it's easy, he can do 30 seconds and add 30-second intervals until he reaches 5 minutes. If this is too much, he can do 30 seconds, rest for 1 minute, another 30 seconds and stop. Now, his minimum to beat is two 30-second repetitions. The point is to start from his current level and build targets by adding small increments. Finally, he needs to track his success in numbers. It's motivating to see one's progress.

Think of the hard thing you noted above and how you might turn this into a goal. Why do goals matter? Goals provide us with direction and help organize and master our time as well as achieve a sense of control. With goals, we have a reason to get up in the morning and tend to try harder, learn better, and get better results. They also pull us towards the future[48] and give us a space in which to retreat when times are tough.

Goals must be enjoyable along the way otherwise you won't stick with them. Select goals to approach rather than avoid. An example is choosing to eat one extra serving of vegetables a day instead of just "not eating junk food". Not doing something keeps you in a state of wanting and that's miserable. At last, set small goals that can be reached within a week. If it's too big yet, break it down and go from there.

Finally, your goal should be realistic, sustainable over time, and personal to you (versus what others think you must do). If you don't engage in physical activity, going for a daily 5-minute walk might be enough until it becomes a habit and then you can add time as you go. For others, this

---

[48] Lutz, R., Karoly, P., & Okun, M. (2008). The why and the how of goal pursuit: Self-determination, goal process cognition, and participation in physical exercise. *Psychology of Sport and Exercise, 9*, 559–575; Headey, B. (2008). Life goals matter to happiness: A revision of set-point theory. *Social Indicators Research, 86*, 213–231.

might be too little and your goal may be to run an hour. Choose what works for you and you only.

Task: Choose two medium term goals and break them into small steps. Then, outline those smaller steps starting from this week onwards. It's okay if you have to adjust the timeline as you go, but don't pick something so far in the future that you'll forget or burnout on the way. And remember that a good goal uses your skills, talents, and learning along the way. An example might be that you want to learn Arabic and be able to ask for basic directions in two months or play the piano and learn a simple song by the fall.

Goal Number 1:

1.

2.

3.

Goal Number 2:

1.

2.

3.

How will I deal with self-defeating thoughts that stop me from attaining my goals?

What's my first step – starting today – to start reaching this goal?

We're Programmed to Get Bored!

When Haitham first started running, ooouf, it was hard; he could barely do a minute. But, over time, he got better and reached 45 minutes. Yet, he started to get bored and eventually quit. It became an unpleasant chore. He felt like a loser for not sticking with it when everyone else clearly loved it!

Remember adaptation, the habituation to negative and positive events? Another way to understand adaptation relates to skills. Haitham adapted because he became good at running. When you become good at something, adaptation is natural. It means there is nothing left to learn, you've done it! Boredom[49] is a signal for you to challenge yourself for continued growth.

Have you adapted to your activities? Which ones?

---

[49] Csikszentmihalyi, M. (2000). *Beyond boredom and anxiety.* San Francisco: Jossey-Bass. (Original work published in 1975)

Think of activities you've done which you really enjoyed but stopped because they got boring.

Stop the boredom!

Here's what you and Haitham can do to push back against adaptation.

1. Expect it. You may love chocolate, but you'd get bored eating it every day. Adaptation is normal.
2. Make it harder. Haitham can increase his incline, speed up, or race against the clock. He can even sign up for long races.
3. Use variety. He can run outside, in a pool, do a slow but steep day and alternate with a fast but downhill day. He can race against friends, or alternate with weights or cycling. He can change his music and listen to radio instead, or run in other neighborhoods with new people.
4. Change the frequency or timing. He can run less, maybe twice a week, so he can miss it. He can change the time at which he runs, i.e., night not morning, or run more than once a day, but with shorter times.

Adaptation is important to know about as many activities that are good for us and help us grow can be wasted for this reason. If you start to get bored, it's not a sign to stop or that the activity isn't for you, it means you're getting good and you need to manage your pathway to excellence otherwise.

What can you do to prevent adaptation? Write your anti-boredom plans here.

Talk to Yourself, but Do It Right!

Beyond setting goals, we can keep ourselves engaged by using self-talk.[50] But, we neither use it well, nor judge the quality of the self-talk and that's a problem because what we say to ourselves has the same impact as others saying it to us. So, if we call ourselves dumb, our feelings follow. Yet, you don't have to pretend all is perfect, we do make mistakes and we're not always at our best. In these cases, aim for realistic self-talk where you accept your mistakes and move forward without floundering under the weight of your judgement. Rehashing mistakes won't change anything. Notice it, make amends if possible, solve it, and move on. The self-talk should end there.

Think of a situation you are facing and consider how your self-talk helps. Does it bring out the best of you or create insecurity or doubt? Create new self-talk that is more positive and functional. You can even practice with different types of self-talk that suit many situations, optimize your excellence, and increase positive emotion. Try the new self-talk this week and record how it went here.

---

[50] Gammage, K.L., Hardy, J., & Hall, C.R. (2001). A description of self-talk in exercise. *Psychology of Sport and Exercise, 2,* 233–247; Hardy, J., Hall, C.R., & Alexander, M.R. (2001). Exploring self-talk and affective states in sport. *Journal of Sports Sciences, 19,* 469–475.

My current self-talk is…

The result of this self-talk…

My better self-talk would sound like…

The likely results of my new self-talk would be…

It's the Opposite of Depression: Flow

Flow[51] is the reward we get from playing sports, music, or engaging in the arts. Anything can bring on flow as long as it is difficult, uses our skills and talent, and requires an investment in time. In flow, we:

- Take control; we are doing, partaking, and responding. We are not just watching life go by.
- Concentrate and think of nothing but the activity. We are narrowly focused and lose track of time.
- Do not worry about our self-image, i.e., hair, or clothes and we let competitors worry about themselves.
- Select difficult tasks and use skills in ways we've not done before or more than usual causing us to grow.
- Respond to feedback that tells us what to do next. We do this by reading and interpreting our activity.
- Consider the activity gratifying and feel excited for it. Flow is rare in activities we are forced into.

Flow only emerges when we develop ability and don't think too much. At first, you'll be self-conscious when you take on any new activity, you're learning; but in time, you'll forget about yourself and focus on doing and being. This brings on flow, where you detach from the world and focus

---

[51] Csikszentmihalyi, M. (1990). *Flow: The psychology of optimal experience*. New York: Harper & Row.

on your experience in the absence of thought. It is the opposite of depression as it forces the mind to be positively occupied. Have you experienced a state of flow before?

How often do you experience it these days?

Doing what?

Some people don't experience flow as they are too self-conscious. Others don't like hard work and prefer an easy life. Others don't see the point. Yet, participating in activity is important because the usual life tests we face versus those we create and direct, do not offer ways to develop our skills as they are inconsistent, random, and at times, painful. We don't learn from them in the same way we learn from weekly tennis matches for example that teach us discipline, focus, confidence, strength, and mastery over our emotions and actions.

If you don't experience flow, discuss why you think this is the case. How can you change your mind about the way in which you engage with life's activities so that you can experience more flow?

Getting flow...

Here are a few questions people have asked about flow which may be helpful to you.

- What activity will being on flow?
  Anything that involves effort, time, skills, and increasing challenge like doing weights, sculpture, playing the violin, writing a novel, or flying a plane! None is easy, but all are possible in time with focus and effort.
- What if I'm not good at anything?
  Everyone has talents; you just don't know yours yet. Give yourself permission to try three new activities, more than once. Don't look for something you're good at, look for something you like and can be good at.
- I've tried something and I'm really not good.
  That's what practice is for. Growth doesn't come from doing something a few times, so give it a good chance. But, sometimes you'll find that you're not good at it and don't like it. Try something else.
- I like what I'm doing, but can't focus. My thoughts wander.
  If you have the mental space to think of the past or present, your activity is too easy. Increase its difficulty, complexity, or intensity to force your focus. Stop thinking; do.

In what activity could you generate flow?

How will you deal with adaptation? How will you increase the challenge in this activity?

How will you deal with overthinking?

Is there is anything else that stops you from being absorbed? What can you do about it?

Too Much, Too Soon

There are other things that interfere with engagement and that is jumping ahead too soon, or having rising aspirations.[52] As we reach goals and attain better circumstances, we invariably and quickly develop greater dreams and aspirations. While this is normal and keeps us wanting more and getting more, it can also result in the inability to enjoy what we have. In effect, we look ahead too soon.

Let's take Shamsa. She joined the Sharrif Corporation three years ago and had big ambitions to move ahead in the company. She is good at her job and frequently recognized. She got her first promotion after eight months in the company and quickly went from being an assistant, to a junior and now to a middle level executive. She has her sights on upper management and works hard to get there. Yet, listen to what she said to her cousin last week at lunch. "Amna, I feel like I haven't accomplished much. I feel I should be further ahead, like I'm not there yet…"

Amna was left speechless as they both started the company at the same time and Amna is still in the same role. "What do you mean you've accomplished nothing? Are you kidding? You've been promoted the most and the most

---

[52] Chancellor, J., & Lyubomirsky, S. (2011). Happiness and thrift: When (spending) less is (hedonically) more. *Journal of Consumer Psychology, 21*, 131–138; Jacobs Bao, K., Layous, K., & Lyubomirsky, S. (2015). Aspirations and well-being: When are high aspirations harmful? Manuscript under review.

quickly and where is 'there' you feel you should be? You wouldn't be happy if you were CEO!"

Amna might have been a little harsh, but she's not wrong. Shamsa's rising aspirations are to blame; the moment she reaches a goal, she already moves to the next and never revels or basks in what she just accomplished. The more she gets, the more she wants, and the less happy she is.

To conquer rising aspirations, she needs to appreciate positive changes well after they occur and find ways to enjoy and engage with the changes so as not to focus too quickly on future goals that can reduce present happiness. She can set her sights on more, but needs to enjoy the ride too; otherwise, what's the point of reaching one's aspirations if they bring no joy along the way?

Do you jump ahead too soon and not make time to enjoy your circumstances or the goals you've reached?

How can you slow your aspirations to get more joy out of what you've accomplished?

Plan It, but Don't Do It!

Maitha and Ibrahim are newly wedded and off to France. Both have been in love with the idea of going to Paris, the city of love, for many years. To prepare for their perfect trip, they take to reading reviews of the best hotels by the Seine, the latest and newest art galleries which they adore and quaint little bistros at which to eat and drink. Maitha has added a few home interior design stores she wants to visit for good measure and Ibrahim has found a few neighborhoods he'd like to walk around in. They've been planning for months and the sense of anticipation is high! Three weeks before their flight, they create a special calendar and mark off the days. Just the thought of being in Paris makes them smile and feel closer to one another.

It's the big day…

They are late getting to the airport due to a flat tire on the way. They make it in time, but not without stress. In the plane, they hit turbulence and Ibrahim feels ill. When things start to settle, a baby starts to cry, and continues for the rest of the flight. When they arrive in Paris, the passport official shouts instructions in French, which neither understand. Their luggage is lost and there is a public transportation strike that started only hours before. Like it couldn't get worse, next to the hotel, which indeed is very nice, construction keeps them up at night. It rains for 5 of the 7 days and Ibrahim's office calls him non-stop. It's not quite the trip they dreamt of, nor is it producing much for positive emotion.

In fact, they are less happy on the actual trip than they were at home thinking about it. This is the problem with reality. It never lives up to expectation and is usually worse than the picture we imagined. Yet, the problem isn't the crying baby or the missing luggage. It's that these things were not in the picture they imagined, which acted as the standard against which they judged the event. If the actual event was better than the picture, they would have been happy, but in this case, because the actual event was less favorable than the picture, they were unhappy. This is more often than not the case, after all who envisions a horrible holiday? But, had they said "let's do Paris and hang out", these things would have been easier to laugh off.

Think about your planned positive experiences; what is most pleasurable, the hours, days, or weeks before it, or the actual event? How something is experienced in reality can fall short of how it was imagined. In fact, having positive experiences can be less enjoyable than just thinking about them,[53] while anticipating future positive experiences can be more enjoyable than reminiscing about past positive experiences.[54]

The key is this: Anticipate as much as you can beforehand to soak up as much positive emotion as possible. Dream about the scenes, possibilities, and various best-case scenarios. Then, stop just before the event and just stay open to whatever happens. See the mental and emotional anticipation as one event and the actual trip as a second event that is entirely unrelated. See things for what they are and create an entirely new experience when you arrive based on what is in front of you.

What's your strategy for dealing with anticipation?

---

[53] Richins, M. L. (2013). When wanting is better than having: Materialism, transformation expectations, and product-evoked emotions in the purchase process. *Journal of Consumer Research, 40*(1), 1–18.

[54] Caruso, E. M., Gilbert, D. T., & Wilson, T. D. (2008). A wrinkle in time: asymmetric valuation of past and future events. *Psychological Science, 19*(8), 796–801.

Pathway of Positive Relationships

Relationships lead to happiness and they all count, family, friends, and even strangers, whom we don't often think about. Consider how you feel when a person holds the door open for you, smiles, and says hello versus when a store clerk doesn't acknowledge you even exist?

First, to which social networks and groups do you belong? No matter how strong (i.e., family, friends) or weak (i.e., neighbors, colleagues, social groups) these ties are, name them as they all matter.

They help us see in the dark.

Relationships provide occasions for friendly competition, the practice of unfamiliar or well-used qualities, and generation of new ideas. The more ties we have, the fuller our personalities become as we use different sides of ourselves to deal with varied people. Relationships also help define who we are. I am a daughter, sister, partner, and friend, but, without relationships, I am just a shell in relation to no one. Connections provide roles and an identity.

In contrast, without people, we lose touch with the boundaries of reality. Imagine you only had yourself to talk to, how would you know if you were inappropriate or exaggerating? The feedback we get from others is critical in coping with the world and disconnecting from others makes our thoughts unravel easily. People provide the limits of reality and we need to be told where those are sometimes.

How do you feel about your connections? Do you connect too much and not have time for you, or not enough and end up talking to yourself all day? What's a good balance?

What do you offer in relationships that makes you a good friend? Do you provide some of the benefits listed? What other benefits are there to being in a relationship with you?

Name It to Improve It!

Sometimes relationships drive us crazy! People have their quirks and while small, they can get in the way of strengthening relationships. Here is an activity you can do to interpret those oddities otherwise.

Naming three good things in relationships is a way to find and focus on the positives. Use this with a close relationship that is strained right now and reflect on the positive characteristics of that person. Or, you can positively reframe behaviors that bother you like the examples below. In the last column, think of how you can share what you see the other person doing well so that they are encouraged to do it more often.

Who?	Good thing	Good thing	Good thing	How to tell them.
Week 1: partner	He always tries to help (even if it's not helpful!).	He's thoughtful in his way, he opens doors for me.	He takes pride in his family, takes interest in our lives.	After supper during our walk, I'll stop and say it.

| Week 2: Teenage daughter | She speaks her mind; this will make her stand up for herself later. | She's an original and doesn't follow the crowd. | She is protective of her sister; family means something. | I'll write a note and leave it in her lunch box. |

Three good things

Who?	Good thing	Good thing	Good thing	How will I share this?

Invest and Make a Date

We can improve relationships by investing time in them, but having the same conversations won't make you closer; in fact, you'll soon adapt and be bored. So, plan a date! It can be a coffee, walking, movie, museum date, or even a gym date with a friend, colleague, or nephew. Move the conversation away from the usual and ask things like: what's your biggest joy in life? Biggest fear? If you weren't afraid, what would you do? The conversation will go to new heights! You can google "conversation starters" for more ideas. Plan three outings in the coming month and call these people right now to reserve their time!

Outing 1. Who will I ask on a date? What will we do? When, where? How can I make it memorable?

Outing 2. Who will I ask on a date? What will we do? When, where? How can I make it memorable?

Outing 3. Who will I ask on a date? What will we do? When, where? How can I make it memorable?

Supersize That Order!

Are there people you've met only once at a conference, wedding, through other friends or a neighbor's house? Why don't you be brave and organize a breakfast of interesting people you hardly know and ask them each to bring a friend? Don't pack the place full of your friends, but go mostly alone so that you too are forced to meet new people. You can even set conversation cards on each plate and put a limit on how long each person sits at one place; one chair for starters, another for desert, a third for tea. With a broad mix, you'll surely find someone with which to connect and you'll be the breakfast queen everyone wants to meet.

Where:

When:

Who:

Capitalization: Share and Show It!

Capitalization[55] refers to how we respond to others' good news and it's a way to increase our happiness. But capitalization also depends on how you share good news too.

What happens when you share good news? Do you get a good response? Are others excited and happy for you? How do you share it? Are you enthusiastic or do you minimize your good news, or not tell it at all?

Maitha got a very lucrative project with the ministry. She worked on the proposal for months and it's her life passion. She'll make good money, but it's more about the interesting research she'll do and that her career will grow. It also means others recognize her work excellence. Maitha feels great and shares the good news.

"Guess what, Aysha? I got that project I've been working on…"

"Wow!" responds Aysha. "Tell me all about it!"

Aysha asks Maitha what she is looking forward to the most and what it means to her. She is curious, extends the

---

[55] Gable, S.L., & Reis, H.T. (2010). Good news! Capitalizing on positive events in an interpersonal context. In M.P. Zanna (Ed.), *Advances in Experimental Social Psychology* (vol. 42, pp. 195–257). San Diego, CA: Elsevier Academic Press.

conversation with questions to show interest and verbally shares her joy. She even copies Maitha's facial expression in empathy. Aysha is using *active-constructive* responding. It's not just listening; it's taking part in the story and constructing positive emotions between herself and Maitha by being curious and showing care. Being happy for other people is one thing, but extending their news and helping them capitalize on their own positive emotions takes relationships to a higher level.

Maitha tries again as she spots Mahmoud. "Remember I told you about the big project I've been working on, well, I got the news; I won the contract!"

"Oh wow, that's great. Good for you. Hey, did you see Jalal go by, I need to ask him something."

Maitha's positive emotions immediately fade given Mahmoud's polite, yet indifferent response. She lost her positivity, but Mahmoud also lost the chance to capitalize on Maitha's emotions for himself. Capitalization is not only for the person sharing the news; it's also for the person hearing it like Aysha who also felt positively as a result of absorbing Maitha's emotions. Capitalization extends positivity for everyone and that's why we should be more mindful of how we share good news as well as respond to that of others.

Am I happy for others? If not, why? What do you think might happen if you were to share in the joy of others? (If this doesn't apply to you, why do you think others don't want to show their joy in response to others good news? Does what they fear actually happen?)

How can I change my responses (expressions, actions, verbal responses, etc.) to the good news of others so that I can get more positive results for myself and deepen my relationships in the process?

Do Good: Forget Yourself

If you want to feel happier and fast, stop tormenting yourself with thoughts and emotions and start doing! Being happy is not only about doing what feels good for you; it equally involves acting in the service of others. In traditional psychology, we often emphasize self-care; doing small things that make you feel good with few consequences, like buying a great pair of shoes. Yet, there are far more powerful actions you can take to boost your happiness.

Doing good deeds allows us to feel good about ourselves, use our character strengths and develop our relationships[56]. It's also a good way not to think of ourselves for a while and can boost our mood as a result. So, rather than trying to change your thoughts or feelings; take an easier route, do a good deed, and focus on everyday things to improve people's lives, like letting someone through in traffic, or complimenting someone. Remember good deeds don't need to cost anything; in fact, the best ones are free.

Who will I select for my good deeds and what can I do? When will I do my good deeds?

---

[56] Aknin, L. B., & Dunn, E. W. (2013). Spending money on others leads to higher happiness than spending on yourself. In J. F. Froh & A. C. Parks (Eds.), *Activities for teaching positive psychology: A guide for instructors* (pp. 93–98). Washington, DC: APA.

Good deed #1:

How did I feel after doing this?

Good deed #2:

How did I feel after doing this?

Good deed #3:

How did I feel after doing this?

Good Deeds Continued...

If you liked the good deed activity, consider keeping it up by creating a regular good deed club with friends or neighbors. Ask everyone for three ideas and go from there. These groups are fun, allow individuals to use their skills and talents, do something meaningful, and feel a sense of purpose. They improve the community and provide a sense of belonging too. Who will you ask? When can you start? You are what the world needs!

Ideas for a good deed club:

Say Thanks, You Won't Be Indebted

There is one more way to improve relationships and it's by saying "Thank you". Because gratitude promotes the savoring of positive experiences and reduces anger and depression,[57] it's a good one to know about.

Select a person who has had a positive influence in your life and write them a letter of gratitude. Let them know what they did and how it made you feel. Handwrite it so that the person has a lasting memory of your thoughts. Once written, meet them in person and read it, or call them and read it. At a minimum, mail it. If the person has passed on, read it to them as though they were here. The closest way to send the message is best.

I know it sounds intimidating. When I do this with my university students, they groan and say, "Miss, no…!" But, they do it and come back with a sprint in their step and a super smile. Be brave: write the letter first and then call.

---

[57] DeWall, C. N., Lambert, N. M., Pond, R. S., Jr., Kashdan, T. B., & Fincham, F. D. (2012). A grateful heart is a non-violent heart: Cross-sectional, experience sampling, longitudinal, and experimental evidence. *Social Psychological and Personality Science, 3,* 232–240. Duckworth, A. L., Steen, T. A., Seligman, M. E. P. (2005). Positive psychology in clinical practice. *Annual Review of Clinical Psychology, 1,* 629–651.

Pathway of Meaning and Accomplishment

Meaning involves the participation in something considered bigger than us, such as volunteering for a regular charity or environmental group. It can also involve our values and religion. Meaning[58] is the glue that connects ideas, objects, and people to one another; in essence, it is the why of what we do and the purpose we give ourselves for taking action. When individuals provide a reason or understanding for why they organize their lives in such a way, purpose emerges.[59] Yet, it is not necessary to have it all figured out or even declare your purpose in life (I'm 41 and still searching!), but it's enough to have a purpose for *right now*, and it can be something like donating blood over the summer months, training for a marathon this term, going to university, or caring for your children. You can change it later.

Meaning even changes in the face of big events like accidents, illness, bombings, or death. Luckily, we are natural meaning makers and ask "why". While this helps us cope, we also need to know when to stop asking why. Sometimes things just happen and other times, things happen for a reason, just not yours. You may have merely been an actor in someone else's story. Find a reasonable explanation and then move on. If it doesn't fit, you'll naturally return to

---

[58] Heine, S. J., Proulx, T., & Vohs, K. D. (2006). The meaning maintenance model: On the coherence of social motivations. *Personality and Social Psychology Review, 10,* 88–110.

[59] Steger, M. F. (2012). Making meaning in life. *Psychological Inquiry, 23,* 381–385.

it anyways. Meaning can emerge at the oddest times too, so stay open to chance.

Alternatively, the pathway of accomplishment is attained by using our skills and efforts toward goals that make us feel effective and involve our achievements yet to come. Sometimes we pursue accomplishments in the absence of positive emotion, meaning, or relationships and do things for no other reason than to say, "Yes, I did it!" We do this to feel skilled and successful. Competition is important here despite its bad reputation and can be used to bring out the best in one another. When I engage in co-opetition with others, we effectively agree to push one another past our limits so that we can grow and experience personal excellence. Being clear on the goal of co-opetition can help attain a sense of achievement even if failure is involved as competing is not actually designed for winning, but to pull the greatness out of us.

What's Important?

Affirming values[60] or redefining purpose involves reminding yourself of who you are, what you stand for, and who is in your life to help you live according to your values and achieve what you want. Thinking about the bigger picture can help to reorient thoughts and actions in line with your beliefs and be useful when you're feeling lost. Reorienting yourself to your own values can even protect you against physical stress.

What are my values? What's important? Examples are hard work, integrity, benevolence, etc. Choose three of your highest values and explain how these emerge in your daily life with family, friends, community, school, or in the workplace.

Who helps you live your best life in accordance with your values?

---

[60] Creswell, J. D., Welch, W. T., Taylor, S.E., Taylor, S. E., & Mann, T. (2005). Affirmation of personal values buffers neuroendocrine and psychological stress responses. *Society, 16,* 846–852.

Is there a situation you're facing that could benefit from you taking actions more in line with who you really are, rather than the person others want you to be? Explain.

Who Is in Your Family Tree?

We can develop meaning by considering where we are from and what our people represent. Think about close and extended family members who, over the course of time and history, overcame adversity with admiration. This activity, sometimes called evoking the ancestor effect, helps convert troubles to optimism, invigorate strengths, and even improve performance.[61] It helps to create meaning from the past and move to the future with confidence.

Describe your family's character strengths, good deeds, and reputation. When people hear your family name, what comes to mind? How are you similar to the people in your extended family? What strengths do you use or could use to be more (or perhaps less) like them? Share what family legacy was passed to you. An idea is to interview family members for these stories or even do it as a family.

---

[61] Fischer, P., Sauer, A., Vogrincic, C., & Weisweiler, S. (2010). The ancestor effect: Thinking about our genetic origin enhances intellectual performance. *European Journal of Social Psychology, 41*(1), 11–16.

Show Your Values!

Are health, religion, your children, family, or learning important? List the things you value greatly in life.

Although we value things like health or learning, we can tell whether these things really matter by looking at our use of time. Does your use of time reflect what matters to you? How did you spend time this week: note where, with whom, and what you were doing to see whether it matches. What changes can you make to live more closely to what you say matters?

Day/Time	Morning	At work	After work	Evening
Sunday				
Monday				
Tuesday				
Wednesday				
Thursday				

Friday		113		
Saturday				

Reverse the Bucket

You may have heard of a "bucket list". It is a mental list on which we note things we'd like to do before it's too late. Items might include: I want to travel to Kenya on safari; I want to jump out of an airplane; I want to open a business or write a novel before I'm 50. Here, I'm interested in what you have already done that stands out in your memory. What have been your accomplishments to date (big or small)? Beside each, write down what it is about you that made it happen.

For example: I learned to play the violin and played my first concert at the age of 23. How did I make it happen? I am dedicated and can resist instant gratification. When all of my friends were having fun, I was practicing. I am also good at blocking out distractions and can focus for long periods of time.

Item 1: …

Item 2: …

Item 3: …

The Real Bucket List

I know you want to do the real thing. It's inspiring and motivating to do a bucket list and fun to dream and anticipate. You've got a long life ahead of you and many days to fill. Most of those will be consumed by work, sleep, and having fun, although these in themselves will be pleasurable and necessary. You will also have lows and highs.

Be purposeful about the time you have; what do you want to accomplish, do, see? Here, only think about the activities you'd want to fill your time with and not how you want to be different; that will come next.

Here are a few examples from my life.

I really want to publish and sell this book – so, if you liked it, don't pass it on, tell your friends to buy it!

I'd like to go to a Viennese ball and wear a big poufy dress and waltz to Vivaldi with a great man (red face!)

I'd like to take a hot air balloon over the African plains.

Oh wow, the anticipation! You get where I'm going. What about you?

My Best Possible Self

Imagining our best possible self[62] helps us think about life goals and plan them. Doing this activity will provide you with a feeling of control and direction and prompt you to take steps to make your best self real. This is the final activity and one that you can and should do many times, as you will need to update your progress and determine new goals as you reach the old ones. You can do this activity on poster boards and write, paint, draw, or make a collage to elicit as much detail as possible about your best self. The activity is in two parts.

Part 1: Think about who you will be when you reach your best possible self at home, work, school, with friends, or other spheres of your life. How will I look? How will my thoughts and actions be different? How will I interact with others? How will I present myself differently? Write your vision first and provide as much detail as possible about the future vision you have of yourself at your best.

Part 2: Now, use the table to complete your best self by pulling some goals from your vision and turning these into actions you can start doing now. Fill in as many boxes that apply and update these over time, as you will reach them and adapt to the activities you are doing to get there. Your steps should be realistic, reachable, and not too far away. At the

---

[62] Sheldon, K.M., & Lyubomirsky, S. (2006). How to increase and sustain positive emotion: The effects of expressing gratitude and visualizing best possible selves. *The Journal of Positive Psychology, 1*(2), 73–82.

end, fill in your current resources that will be helpful to you in reaching your goals.

Part 1: My Best Self
(Write it here)

Part 2: Best Self Goals

Family	Work	Social/ Friends	Community
Health/ Fitness	Environment	Religion/ Spirituality	Education
Recreation/ Hobbies	Finances	Travel /Learning	Contribution to world
Other			
Current resources (friends, family, health, skills, talents, smarts, money, time, etc.)			

The Road Ahead

Congratulations! You've worked really hard and changed how you think, act, and even what you focus on. Others have noticed your changes too.

Remember your self-efficacy: your ability to make happiness happen for yourself? Has it changed?

1	5	10
I'm awful at making happiness happen.	I can do it sometimes, I just don't know how I do it!	I'm awesome and know how to keep it there.

I'm sure this score has changed. You made that happen all by yourself by reading, putting in effort, thinking about the ideas, and taking part in every single activity. That deserves a round of applause! Woo Hoo!

Before we end, I have a little bit more to say.

- Continue to partake in these strategies. You can reread this book a million times and rewrite your answers elsewhere. You'll also see how much you've changed by reading your old answers.
- Be mindful of adaptation. Although I encourage you to repeat the strategies, mix them up, do them with other people, or in different contexts so that they don't get boring and you give up.
- Don't be afraid of hard work. It's what makes us who we really are.

- Know that you will be laughed at if it hasn't happened already. When others aren't happy, the last thing they want to be around is someone who is! Don't take it personally.
- You'll still be unhappy sometimes. It means you're normal. Go ahead and be unhappy, but know when enough is enough and when you decide it's time to move on from being unhappy, do it. Whatever you do, don't pressure yourself to be happy, it'll backfire and your unhappiness will last even longer.

OK, my friend, I think this is where I leave you to live your amazing, super delicious, oversized life!

Go well, live large, and dream big.

Dr. Louise Lambert

www.ingramcontent.com/pod-product-compliance
Lightning Source LLC
Chambersburg PA
CBHW050538160726
48003CB00002B/651